OAK NOTEBOOK

ROBIN HARFORD

1

INTRODUCTION

From the oak forests of Europe to the tropics of the Americas, around 500-600 species of oak can be found.

The oak covered one third of Europe during the reign of England's King Henry VII (1457-1509), but these ancient forests have all but vanished due to logging.

Of all the mighty oaks in the world, the English oak or common oak (*Quercus robur*), also called the pedunculate oak, brown oak, truffle oak or European oak, is of particular importance to European mythology.

It is *Q. robur* that is described here unless otherwise indicated.

Along with the ash and yew, which had great significance to the mother goddesses. The oak was an important figure of the father gods and took its place among the supreme trees used in magic and ritual.

Oak is both a humble tree and a royal figure. It has inspired humans throughout the ages with its steadfast trunk and widely outstretched branches.

It was at once the tree of kings and a tree of peasants. King Arthur's round table was said to be made from a single slice of oak, while at the same time children in Ireland would catch a falling oak leaf for good luck.

Oak's unique story in plant lore was as the great patriarch of the forest.

2

_____

FOOD

Acorns have long been valued as a special food - a gift from the oak gods. The ancient Greeks considered the oak to be the first tree that fell to earth to bring mankind the riches of acorns and honey.

While some classic authors described early inhabitants of Greece and southern Europe, living in primeval forests, as being fat on the fruits of the oak. Folkard tells us: "These primitive people were called *Balanophagi* (eaters of Acorns)".

An English chronicler wrote in the 17th century:

> *Acorns...(before the use of Wheat-Corn was found out) were heretofore the Food of Men, nay of Jupiter himself ... till their Luxurious Palats were debauched ... And Men had indeed Hearts of Oak; I mean, not so*

hard, but health, and strength, and liv'd naturally,
and with things easily parable and plain.

J Russell Smith suggests that historically humans may have eaten more acorns than wheat and that acorns were of great importance to hunter-gatherers, before the era of agriculture:

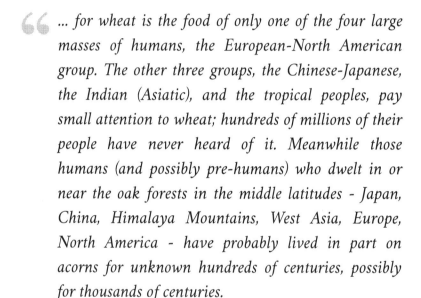 *... for wheat is the food of only one of the four large masses of humans, the European-North American group. The other three groups, the Chinese-Japanese, the Indian (Asiatic), and the tropical peoples, pay small attention to wheat; hundreds of millions of their people have never heard of it. Meanwhile those humans (and possibly pre-humans) who dwelt in or near the oak forests in the middle latitudes - Japan, China, Himalaya Mountains, West Asia, Europe, North America - have probably lived in part on acorns for unknown hundreds of centuries, possibly for thousands of centuries.*

A resurgence of interest in acorns - and the oak as a 'bread and butter tree' - occurred during the food shortages of the World Wars where it was 'rediscovered' that acorns could be added to flour to make nutritious 'acorn bread'. Acorns are easily prepared at home and provide high oil and starch content that is easily digested.

Nutritionally, these nuts of the oak tree provided a very

valuable source of food for early people. Arthur Haines writes:

> *[The nut] contains starches, oils, some protein, the minerals calcium, phosphorus, and potassium, as well as several B complex vitamins (unfortunately, the B vitamins are water soluble and will largely be lost in the final product). The protein is high quality protein due to its completeness.*

François Couplan suggests bitter acorns contain 4% protein, 4% fats, 30-35% starch, 10% sugars, and 5-10% tannins and minerals.

Small amounts of tannins have an antioxidant effect. Tannic acid (tannin) is a water-soluble polyphenol that is present in tea, green tea, coffee, red wine, nuts, fruits and many plant foods.

Is it possible to eat acorn or acorn products without first leaching off the tannins and reducing the bitterness?

For myself, leaching is compulsory.

Too much tannin can impact your kidneys and liver. As the old adage says: "The dose makes the poison".

Personally I value my internal organs, so I spend quite a bit of time leeching out the tannin. You'll find instructions on how to do this under the 'Recipe' section.

There are reports of dried and milled acorn used in Estonia, on occasion, without special leaching processes to improve the flavour. This usage was rare.

Euell Gibbons in Stalking the wild asparagus recalls foraging for acorns from the different species of oaks in North America, and found them "considerably improved" after roasting, although his experience convinced him that "even unleached acorns of some species are worth the attention of anyone who is really hungry".

Haines provides several forager-tips for collecting acorns, including allowing the first crop that fall from the trees in autumn to remain on the ground, "[they] are generally immature or damaged by some pathogen", and waiting for larger quantities to fall in the second crop later in the month.

Vigilance is also required against pests of acorns that ruin the nuts in many foragers' crops. To separate the wheat from the chaff, so to speak, observe the attached cup (which should detach easily if the acorn is not infected), finding exit holes of grubs, avoiding dull brown or grey acorns likely to be old nuts from the past season, finding darkened areas, dark spots or a rippled bottom on bad acorns, or noticing whether the shell has slipped away from the nut.

In other words, inspect your wild edibles as closely as you would fruit or vegetables selected from your vegetable patch, the supermarket or market - use your common sense.

Finally, a float test will determine whether an acorn is good or bad - simply put the acorns in a bowl of water and discard those that float to the top. Once the best acorns have been selected, it's good to prepare them quickly for eating, cooking or storage (such as by drying) as the raw nuts have a short shelf life.

Acorn kernels were sometimes leached by burying in ash or charcoal and watered to leach out the bitter tannins. This method was used by Native American Indian tribes to prepare acorns gathered from their own native oak species. Among some tribes, ground acorns were placed in a hollow pocket of sand with water trickling through to release the bitterness. As a result, the acorn meal was sometimes eaten with sand and caused teeth to be 'sandpapered' down.

Alternatively, acorns can be boiled in several changes of water to reduce the bitterness, which is kinder to teeth. My colleague Francois Couplan suggests any bitterness that remains in the 'acorn mush' can be resolved by mixing with milk. The mush can be spread on a baking sheet and baked in the oven to make a hardened meal to be stored for months, or mixed with flour.

Anything that could be used to make flour was a valuable commodity for early people. Flour provided the means to make bread when other foods were scarce. Acorns could be dried and ground into flour and, once again, "with the flour first washed in hot water to remove the tannins and bitter flavour".

Acorn meal, despite being seen as a 'famine food', makes an excellent mix in flour for bread and cakes. My friend Toni

Spencer (definitely an acorn Queen) makes all manner of delicious scrumminess from acorn flour. You are only limited by your imagination, and a bit of experimenting!

Acorn meal can also be added as a bulking agent to soups, stews and even burgers. The flour doesn't necessarily need to be reserved for 'famine bread' either, but could be added to recipes for cakes, muffins, waffles and other baked goods.

Acorns of different *Quercus spp.* have been used for food since prehistoric times and though many culinary uses can be attributed to different species, the uses are perhaps interchangeable between each one.

Some Native American Indian people have eaten acorns raw like chestnuts or candied the nuts like sweets. Canadian indigenous peoples resorted to various species of oak for their fruits and leaves. The acorns were gathered from the ground in autumn by women and children for a variety of uses, such as snacking, roasting, boiling or drying into meal to add to other dishes.

Cooked acorns were sometimes mashed and eaten with animal grease or added to duck broth. A trend with American foragers is to use the cooked nuts for muffin batter or caramelised for candy. Similar uses can be applied to acorns gathered from oak species in Britain, Ireland and Europe as well.

Not to say our own common oak (*Q. robur*) has not been well employed as a wild edible. In Provence and Italy, acorns are mixed with dried figs to make a speciality bread. In Basque regions of Spain, it was common to eat acorns raw, roasted or ground into flour.

In Arab countries, a traditional dish called *racahout* is made from acorns, cocoa, honey, sugar or starch to 'fatten women'.

Children in Estonia snacked on acorns - raw or fire cooked - and ate oak galls or licked the nectar from the leaves. Polish children also enjoyed raw or roasted acorns as a snack up until the early 20th century.

Finely-chopped acorns may be used as a substitute for almonds in most recipes, such as biscuits, flapjacks, baked goods and fish. Acorns also provide a source of a manna called *diarbekei* that is used in butter for cooking. It apparently tastes 'saccharine and agreeable'.

Roasted acorns have been used as a coffee substitute, being chopped and roasted, then ground up, chopped and roasted again, until they provide a suitable blend in countries such as Germany, Estonia, Poland, and the Czech Republic; in the latter, acorns have also provided a cocoa substitute.

In Germany, this is sometimes called '*eichel kaffee*' or acorn coffee. Acorn coffee was also recommended during the Second World War during food shortages.

From the nuts to the leaves and wood. Oak leaves can be used to make wine. In the Czech Republic, oak leaves were an ingredient added to spirits. In Estonia, oak was used to spice beer-like drinks and the bark was sometimes used for vodka flavouring. Oak wood staves for barrels were also used to impart an oaky flavour, from the plant tannins, into beers, wines and spirits.

In the Baltics, Memal oak barrels contribute vanilla-cognac flavour to wine, which is highly rated by the Coopers Guild of England.

In France, wine-flavoured oak shavings from barrels may be used to smoke foods at barbecues. Similar uses occur in different oak species, such as North America's white oak (Q. alba) which is used in barrels to mature whisky.

Oak charcoal has been used to smoke fish for flavouring as well. Finally, an unusual use for oak leaves in Estonia and Poland was as an additive to lactofermented cucumbers, which made the cucumbers dark.

If you can find no other use for oak leaves in your kitchen, despite all these ideas, you can bake bread on oak leaves to stop the bottoms from burning.

Amongst all these numerous and innovative uses for oak as a wild edible, it's also recognised that species like our English oak (Q. robur) was an emergency source of nutrition when times required it.

Even the trunk of the tree has provided an edible source of gum. In Poland, acorn meal was added to bread as famine food up until the 20th century or used to flavour bread. In the Czech Republic, the flowering buds of oak were ground into flour during times of scarcity.

In Spain and Italy, around 20% of the food of poorer people once consisted of acorns. A French bishop of the 9th century had asked his priests to make sure his people had plenty of acorns during a food shortage. In Portugal and again in Majorca "roasted acorns are eaten exactly as one eats roasted chestnuts in America."

Across the globe the oak provides diverse delicacies. The sawtooth oak (*Q. acutissima*) provides *dotori muk* or acorn curd, which is eaten as a summer 'cooling' food with chilis, green onions and soy sauce. It's usually sold in Korean markets.

In Japan, the leaves of the daimyo oak (*Q. dentata*) are wrapped around festive rice cakes called kashiwa mochi; *Q. aliena* acorns are also ground into flour for dumplings. The dead-wood of another species in Japan, *Q. glandulifera*, is used to grow the shiitake mushroom.

In south-west Asia, the acorns of the holm oak (*Q. ilex*) are mixed with clay to make a cake or bread resembling soft chocolate or nougat. This delicacy is eaten with lard, milk, cheese or honey. In Mongolia, leaves of *Q. mongolica* are gathered to make a tea, brewed with Siberian crabapple fruit. In Tibet, the resin of *Q. lanata* is boiled in water to make tea.

The acorns of the white oak (*Q. alba*) of North America are eaten oven-baked with butter and salt, or cooled as a salty 'nut' treat. The swamp white oak (*Q. bicolor*) yields particularly large acorns in comparison to other oak species. These can be ground into meal for bread and cakes or other baked goods. In California, the wood of the coast live oak (*Q. agrifolia*) is preferred for smoking foods such as steaks and chicken in Santa Maria-style barbecues. The acorns were also ground into meal for bread and soups.

In eastern-north America, the oak galls produced by gall wasps on species, such as the red, black and scarlet oaks, were picked by children to suck out the sweet juice. The live oak (*Q. virginiana*) is said to yield very sweet acorns from which an edible oil is obtained by crushing and boiling the nuts in water, then skimming off the oil from the surface.

For Native American Indian tribes, such as the Dakota, Iroquois, Ojibwa, Omaha, Pawnee, Ponca and Potawatomi, *Q. rubra* provided an important food source. The Italian oak (*Q. cerris*) of Eurasia is harvested for a 'manna-like' substance called gaze, which is collected from the branches and boiled to reduce into syrup. The syrup may be mixed with flour to make a sweetmeat or used to sweeten other foods. It is also mixed with oak leaves to make a type of cake. In parts of Spain, the acorns of cork oak (*Q. suber*) are fed to pigs bred for gourmet pork products, such as chorizo, to give the meat a distinctive flavour.

Around 50 species of oak are listed as a world economic plant with their acorns as a nutritious wild edible, suggesting the species is as important to us now as it once was to early people. Smith in his Tree Crops, published in 1929, asked whether the acorn had the wonderful quality of a factory food, while being easily and naturally preserved in storage.

Could it be mixed with cereals or become a nut butter as popular as peanut? Then, of course, there is the tannin:

> *How easy for the chemical engineer to get it out if he had 50,000 tons of acorns a year to deal with! Tannin is worth money. We scour the ends of the world for it. It is quite possible that income from tannin might put a premium price on bitter acorns.*

He called for "oak orchards" with their crops of acorn cereals to be grown on hills "now washing away as we plow them". Thus, the oak is still a supreme wild edible worldwide in all its guises.

3

MEDICINE

As a magical tree, the oak was believed to have the power to heal through all manner of peculiar rhymes and remedies, none of which impressed German mystic Hildegard of Bingen (1098-1179). She was rather scathing about the oak:

> *The Oak is cold, hard and bitter. It is a symbol of ruin. Oak wood and acorns are useless as medicine. Its fruit can also not be eaten by men; but some bent-backed animals such as swine feed themselves on them and become fat.*

She didn't mention the sympathetic properties of the tree - for the oak, like the ash, fell into a category of trees whereby a person could transfer their sickness to it and be cured. In the tradition of 'split-cure' trees, people crawled between a gap between two oaks that had grown together, or used the bark as a 'nail tree' to stick their suffering to the oak.

English diarist John Evelyn (1620-1706) recalled the belief that sleeping under an oak tree "will cure paralysis, and recover those whom the malign influence of the Walnut-tree has smitten".

The mistletoe that grew on the oak had many magical and medical uses. But that is the story of the mistletoe. Indeed, the oak was thought to bestow magical healing properties to any other plants growing on its trunk or branches, such as the polypody fern.

English herbalist John Gerard wrote on the topic of oak galls:

> ... *that which growth on the bodies of olde Okes is preferred before the rest: in steede of this most do use that which is found under the Okes, which for all that is not to be termed Quercinum, or Polypodie of the Oke.*

He recommended these galls be ground in white wine vinegar to treat skin problems or to yield a black hair dye. The tannic acid in oak products was also said to produce a decoction for blackening hair.

All parts of the oak - wood, bark, leaves, acorns and gallnuts (the latter being swollen balls caused by parasitic infection of the tree, usually formed by wasps) - were used in folk remedies since the Hippocratic Schools of medicine.

Many authors followed the words of Dioscorides (50 AD) who described the tree's astringent and dehydrating properties, and the binding and haemostatic (stopping the flow of blood) qualities of its bark.

Pliny the Elder (77 AD) also wrote about the leaves, 'berries' and bark of the oak in decoctions as an all-round antidote. He crushed acorns mixed with salt and grease from a wagon axle to cure malignant scleroses.

Oak galls had an even wider range of use from treating mouth diseases, infected eyes and ears, toothache, stomach disorders, dysentery, rashes, abscesses, skin ailments and burns, swollen spleens and regulating menses.

Oak charcoal was crushed and mixed with honey to cure anthrax, although given oak was a supreme tree in the days of the ancient Greeks and Romans, which no one dare harm, one wonders where all this oak charcoal was made available from.

The classic uses of oak developed further in the Middle Ages as herbalists made more use of the leaves, acorns and galls.

Flemish healer Rembert Dodoens (1517-1585), or Dodonaeus, wrote:

> *Oak galls stop pain and are useful against bloody excrement or diarrhoea ... Gallnuts are also useful against the softening and swelling of the gums, any swelling of the tonsils and the throat, as well as sores in the mouth. Gallnuts also stem women's flow and make a dropped uterus return to its place...Gallnuts ... soak in vinegar or water, will dye the hair black and eliminate proud flesh ... Ash of gallnuts mixed with vinegar and wine stops every kind of flow and bleeding.*

On the Greek island of Chios, oak galls in wine were used to treat diarrhoea.

English physician Nicholas Culpeper (1616-1654) described the bark, leaves and acorns in his Complete Herbal of 1653. Like Dodonaeus, he recommended the oak as a 'binding' medicine that helps to stem bleeding and vomiting, and which "resists the poison of venomous creatures" as well as "the force of poisonous herbs and medicines".

He described the distilled water of oak buds as a remedy for inflammation, pestilence, burning fevers, liver complaints and kidney stones. He also wrote: "The water that is found in the hollow places of old Oaks, is very effectual against any foul or spreading scabs."

Dutchman Abraham Munting (1626-1683) even praised the moss that grows on oaks for "soaked in beer, and laid between cloths on the breasts of a woman, will heal these if they are swollen".

Folk records describing the oak as a medicinal plant - in absence of all magic - are still held in living memory for curing mild ailments such as diarrhoea or ringworm. Plant folklorist Roy Vickery reports: "Diarrhoea: grate a ripe acorn into warm milk and give to patient. [Taylor MSS, Woolverstone, Suffolk]."

Ground acorns in milk were another remedy for diarrhoea, grated acorns in white wine were said to cure a stitch, and roasted acorns with cinnamon were good for a rupture (perhaps meaning a hernia). Vickery also provides us with: "Ringworm: get six leaves of an oak tree, boil them and drink the water in which they are boiled. [IFCSS MSS 800: 219, Co. Offaly]."

Further back in time, Greek physician Avicenna wrote that the Persians inhaled smoke from the burning wood of our English oak (Q. robur) to relieve diarrhoea and to reduce pain.

The bark of the oak was seen to be the most practical part of the tree in folk medicine, despite the oak galls being widely praised. An infusion of the bark was used to treat rheumatism.

In the Scottish Highlands, oak bark infusion was gargled for mouth diseases and sore throats; the twigs might also be used for toothbrushes.

In Ireland, the bark was used for ailments such as toothache, ulcers and as a treatment for hardening the feet in summertime. David Allen and Gabrielle Hatfield suggest oak was used more in Irish folk medicine than British:

> *Collected in spring from branches four to five years old, dried, chopped up and then boiled, this has been valued as a gargle for sore throats in Sligo and Tipperary, to counter diarrhoea in Meath and for adding to a hot bath for sore or excessively perspiring feet (Donegal, Meath, Kilkenny) or a sprained ankle (Offaly).*

Other uses for oak as a medicinal tree in Ireland included for neuralgia, ringworm and pin-worm.

In various folk remedies, not specifically Irish this time, the tannic acid in oak materials were also recommended for sunburn, freckles and pimples, or for complaints such as eczema.

In Suffolk, England, acorns were mixed with beer and gin to cure ague (a shivering fever) or powdered acorns used to treat diarrhoea. In Wales, oak bark mixed with the magic of Midsummer's Day (the piece of bark was rubbed on the left hand in silence) was thought to cure open sores.

Native American tribes have used different species of oak in their folk remedies for generations, including *Q. alba, Q. lobata, Q. velutina,* and *Q. rubra.* The latter, for example, was eaten to treat acute diarrhoea by the Cherokee, Malecite, Micmac, Ojibwa and Potawatomi. A compound derived from the leaves of the swamp white oak (*Q. bicolor*) was also smoked by the Iroquois tribe and exhaled through their noses to relieve catarrh.

It was the tannins in oak that gave it the astringent and 'binding' properties so valued by early herbalists.

Today oak may be recommended as an internal or external medicine for various disorders from wounds, ulcers, chilblains, piles, diarrhoea, dysentery, colitis and general stomach complaints to sore throats, mouth inflammations, tonsillitis, and nasal polyps.

The bark is said to be antiseptic and so useful as a gargle for ailments such as throat infections. The bark has also been used as a substitute to quinine to help treat a fever.

As a cream or ointment, or simply the powdered bark, oak may be helpful for various inflammatory skin diseases such as eczema, bruises, ulcers, chilblains and increased sweating, as well as rashes, itchy skin or scaly skin. Try an oak footbath for sweaty feet too. Thomas Bartram also recommends lint soaked in oak decoction for acute eye complaints.

James (Jim) Duke who was Frank Cook's mentor (Frank was a world-renowned botanical explorer and also my plant mentor), wrote in his Handbook of Medicinal Herbs on oak's medical actions: anti-inflammatory (helpful for problem skin), antiperspirant (footbath for sweaty feet), antiviral (tackles sore throats), and antitumour - as well as anticarcinogenic.

He indicates the tree in herbalism for all the above uses, but also indicates certain types of cancer. Indeed, research has shown that the cork oak (*Q. suber*) may have anticancer activity. However, it's advisable that you always check with your doctor before taking a herbal medicine to complement treatment for any serious condition or disease.

Oak is approved by the Commission E for coughs or bronchitis, diarrhoea, mouth inflammations and skin problems (inflammation), which are largely the uses for which it is prescribed in herbal medicine.

In subtle medicine concerned with maintaining physical and emotional health through the harmony of the body's energy, oak is one of the Bach Flower Remedies. It is taken to "support brave and strong people who never give up the fight, in connection with their health or everyday affairs, but who do not know how or when to give up and who have difficulty acknowledging their weaknesses".

Looking at the medicinal uses of oaks worldwide there are common themes, though it's worth noting: *Q. lanata* in Tibet is chosen for its bark (applied for sprains) and resin (applied externally for muscular aches and pains or taken internally as a powder for bloody dysentery). Manandhar writes, "A paste of cotyledon [the first leaves of a seedling] is applied to scorpion bites."

The astringent properties of oak tannins are found in different species, including *Q. alba*, which is used by some Native American tribes as a bark decoction for stomach pains. Acorns are also considered astringent and the mould that sometimes forms on acorn meal has antibiotic properties, according to Couplan.

4

CAUTIONS

Conway warns the astringency of oak may decrease the nutrients absorbed from our diet if taken in excess. He recommends taking oak internally for complaints such as diarrhoea for no more than three to four days. Oak tannins may damage the mucous membranes of the digestive system.

Kuhnlein and Turner warn that high intakes of tannin, such as are found in oak leaves and acorns, have been linked to some types of cancer. They suggest eating the foliage - bark, shoots and leaves - of oak can be poisonous, and that acorns should be properly leached first.

Topical use may irritate people who suffer from eczema, despite being recommended for eczema in herbal medicine, and in cases of damaged skin.

While there are no known contraindications to taking oak as a medicinal plant or wild edible in relation to drug or supplement interaction, for people with specific medical conditions, or during pregnancy and breastfeeding, this is not proof of its safety. Remember to consult your doctor.

5

FOLKLORE

The oak is one of the highest-ranking trees in the pantheon of Greek, Roman, Celtic, Germanic and Norse mythologies.

It is ruled by Zeus, Jupiter, Thunor and Thor or Donar.

In some legends concerning the origin of Zeus, he was born on Mount Lycaeus, in Arcadia, fed by nymphs from the water of the Nedas stream and worshipped in an oak forest.

The oak was also one of the Seven Noble Trees in Irish traditions. Its royal status sets it apart in folklore as the king of the trees, not unlike the lion as the king of the beasts.

It's unclear whether the tree's importance in ancient rituals came before or after it developed into the oak-god, but the oak was worshipped as a divine power by many ancient peoples.

The word for oak in Irish and in Welsh meant 'chief', signifying the rank in which the tree was held.

The most famous oak in Irish legend was the Oak of Mugna, which was linked with kingship.

Many Celtic folktales associate the tree with other 'royal' animals, such as the stag or the bull.

In antiquity the oak was sometimes called *Quercus Jovis* reflecting its supreme status as the tree of Zeus or Jupiter, king of the gods and husband of Hera or Juno.

Just as the mighty oak spreads its far-reaching branches across the sky, so Zeus ruled the entire span of the heavens and could be felt through the thunder and rain.

A shrine to Jupiter on Capitoline Hill, one of the Seven Hills of Rome, is thought to have stood within an oak forest; a shrine would have stood for his wife Juno on the hill across from the Capitol.

Roman kings wore oak-leaf crowns to associate themselves with the divine tree and its god Jupiter.

During the conversion to Christianity, Juno's shrine became a church of Santa Maria-in-Araceli, meaning 'Mary at heaven's altar'.

St Columba also worshipped the oak at his monastery, possibly located on the island of Iona around 563 AD, built near an oak forest.

The royal oak courted other deities: Rhea, the Titaness mother of the Olympian gods; Demeter or Ceres, goddess of the fruitful earth; Heracles or Hercules, the demi-god hero son of Zeus; Aria, the Arcadian goddess of the Cork Oak; and the Greek Dioscuri, twins Castor and Pollux who took refuge inside a hollow oak. In the case of the latter, many stories are told about a hollow oak.

In a similar myth, Philonome bore twin sons of Ares, called Lycastus and Parrhasius, but threw them into the River Erymanthus. The river god swept the twins to a hollow oak to be nursed by a she-wolf. They were eventually discovered by the shepherd Tyliphus, who brought them home with him.

The tale has parallels to the story of Romulus and Remus, the legendary twin founders of Rome.

Next beneath the gods were kings and heroes.

In Greece and Rome, a person of high-standing or a representation of their figure, such as a statue, might wear oak wreaths or crowns.

For example, the statues of Zeus at Dodona were crowned with acorn-bearing branches, and the victory statue at Herculaneum held an oak wreath in its hand.

In ancient Rome, wreaths were distributed to worthy individuals and it was thought the highest honour went to the person who was presented with an oak wreath.

Julius Caesar (100-44 BC) was awarded an honourable oak wreath by the senate. In time, the oak wreath became a symbol of imperial mercy. The custom of the oak wreath was echoed in Austria where men once stuck oak twigs on their hats or helmets to signify loyalty, power or triumph.

It was forbidden to harm many sacred trees in ancient times, but the oak was judged to be exalted above all and some sources suggest that those who damaged a holy oak in Greece or Rome may have faced execution.

Similarly, in Saxony it was forbidden by law to damage an oak, and in Ostrogothic traditions, all trees but the hazel and the oak could be felled.

Even in the 17th-18th centuries, cutting down an oak was thought to bring bad luck. A story about the felling of the Mile Oak near Oswestry, in Shropshire, England, in 1824 tells of disaster that followed, including fire and sickness.

In Heller, Germany, an oak once grew in a meadow from which it was forbidden even to pick a leaf or burn a twig in the fireplace.

Many British legends imply oak resents being cut, one version being if you cut an oak that you will hear it scream and soon be dead yourself.

The holiness of the oak is probably best described in the myth of Erysichthon, who scorned the gods and wanted to fell the favourite oak of Ceres.

A faithful man tried to stop the crime but Erysichthon killed him and cut down the oak, which fell with a groan.

Ceres called upon the goddess of vengeance to afflict the man with insatiable hunger till nothing could satisfy him. Erysichthon lost his fortune, sold his daughter into slavery, and mutilated his body, but still could not relieve his terrible hunger.

As one of the creator trees, along with the ash and the elm, the Greeks believed the oaks were both the first mothers and host to the forefathers of humankind - the gods who lived within the tree.

In Greek Arcadia, people believed they had originated from oaks. In Scandinavia, the oak sometimes replaced the ash as the tree that the gods used to create the first man.

The Roman poet Virgil (70-19 BC) wrote that the first Romans sprung from the trunks of the oak. When Zeus and Hermes visited earth in disguise as ordinary humans they were turned away from every house in town. Finally, an old couple Philemon and his wife Baucis gave them shelter.

The gods sent a flood to punish the townspeople, but spared the old couple. When they died, Philemon was transformed into an oak and Baucis into a lime tree so that they could grow side-by-side forever.

It's interesting to note that the oak tree itself symbolises 'hospitality' in the language of flowers.

The floods in Boeotia were believed to be caused by Zeus and Hera quarrelling. When the king and queen of the gods stopped fighting, the rain ceased and an oak statue apparently appeared as a symbol of reconciliation between the two.

Plant lore features heavily in Greek and Roman mythology, but the oak was held in particularly high esteem. While the ash was worshipped as the World Tree in many cultures, a conduit that united the realms of the heavens, earth and the underworld, the oak itself was home to a mythical realm of nymphs and animals.

Creatures such as cicadas, bees and the black woodpecker rapping messages to the gods on its bark, were thought to come from the magical oak realm. The Romans also believed in an oak-nymph called Egeria who ruled over the oak forests.

For every leaf that falls from an oak, there seems to be story about the tree in the myths of Greece and other cultures.

Homer's Iliad describes the Trojans encounter with two heroes at the Greek camp:

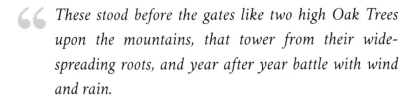 *These stood before the gates like two high Oak Trees upon the mountains, that tower from their wide-spreading roots, and year after year battle with wind and rain.*

In the 2nd century, the Roman Maximus of Tyre observed that the Celts worshipped a tall oak as their supreme deity.

This was the oak-god Esus. The Druids, who practised many rituals beneath the oak, would wear oak-leaf crowns.

The worshippers of Esus believed that everything the oak produced - from the acorns to the parasitical mistletoe that wrapped itself around the tree - was a gift from heaven.

Pliny the Elder (77 AD) wrote on the subject of Celtic oak veneration:

> *The Druids...consider nothing to be holier than the Mistletoe and the tree upon which it grows, on the condition that the tree is an Oak.*
>
> *In addition to this, they choose oak woods as holy woods and will not perform a single ritual act without oak leaves, so that the name of the Druids can be considered as being a Greek name, having been derived from their veneration for the Oak.*
>
> *For they believe that everything that grows upon this tree is sent from heaven, and is a sign chosen by the god himself. Mistletoe only rarely grows on an Oak, but if some is discovered, the Druids gather it with great solemnity.*

A darker side to the cult of the oak was the human sacrifices practised by the Druids.

De Cleene and Lejeune write:

> *The Druids usually held their services in the shadow of a mighty Oak; when offering human sacrifices, the victims were wreathed with oak leaves. The peculiar baskets in which they were offered were made from oak branches, and the wood of the tree was also used for the sacrificial fire.*

Gauls "not rich enough to sacrifice humans" would fasten small offerings to the tree's branches to invoke the blessing of the oak-god Esus, such as protection from plague.

In the Scottish Highlands, it was said a man who was burned for an evil deed would have faggots of green oak kindle the fire.

In Ireland, the oak was dedicated to the god Dagda. The oak was the most important tree in Irish literature, especially next to the ash and the yew.

The ancient Britons also associated the oak with their god of thunder, Taranis, and the god of fire, Baal.

An interesting aspect of Celtic oak-worship is that it can trace the spread of these beliefs to the east.

When Celtic conquerors (Galatians) settled in Asia in the 3rd century, they took the oak-god with them. A small city in Asia Minor was called Drynemetum, a Celtic name meaning 'holy oak forest' or 'temple of the oak'.

Galatians also established oak forests, a dunemeton, on newly taken land. Bologna, in Italy, was once occupied by the Celts, who set up an oak cult. Traces of the cult remained in the 14th century when religious ceremonies took place in the presence of an ancient oak, and children wore wreaths of olive and oak.

Germanic races respected the oak as the tree of the thunder god Thor or Donar, one of their most important gods, and as a tree sacred to other deities, such as the tribal god Teutates or Teutonis.

In the Baltic states, oak was once again dedicated to the gods of thunder, lightning, rain and the heavens.

This is a common theme in plant lore, among such tall and imposing trees that were seen to attract lightning during a storm, although particularly so with the oak.

It was thought the gods showed their favour for the tree by touching it with a lightning flash.

In Latvia, the oak was sacred to the thunder god Perkons, often depicted as a golden oak or 'sun tree'.

In Lithuania, the oak belonged to the thunder god Perkunas who was represented by an eternal flame. Men made sacrifices to the oak god to ensure a good harvest and women gave offerings to the mistletoe, which was seen as connected to the oak's magic.

This overlap of beliefs was common among European

countries, for example, among Slavic races the oak falls under the auspices of the supreme god Perun, a deity of thunder similar to Zeus and Jupiter.

In Estonia, the tree was dedicated to Taara, the supreme god of thunder or the 'Ancient Father'.

In Finland, people believed in a cosmic oak called Taaras whose golden branches spanned the universe. The Finnish saga Kalevala tells of its origin. A dwarf emerged from the sea and became a giant who uprooted an oak, planted by the son of the sun.

The story reflects the golden dawn (or golden branches of the oak) which are chased away by the sun (the dwarf-giant) each morning.

Turning the next page of oak's story, we find that the king of the plant kingdom finds its way into much common folklore concerned with fortune telling, fertility and protective charms.

As Richard Folkard said: "To do full justice to the legendary lore connected with the Oak, it would be necessary to devote a volume to the subject: the largest, strongest, and as some say, the most useful of the trees of Europe, it has been generally recognised as the king of the forest, 'Lord of the woods, the long-surviving Oak.'"

Sadly, I cannot devote volumes to all the folklore and fairy tales told about the oak.

Instead, here is a summary of the themes it shares in common with other plants and trees.

Trees with branches outstretched to the heavens were seen as symbols of life or omens of death - for 'dropping a branch' could certainly cause a serious injury.

One story that reflects both aspects of these beliefs is the Edgewell Tree, an oak that grows close to Dalhousie Castle, near Edinburgh, in Scotland.

The Edgewell Tree was believed to drop a branch when a member of the family died. In July 1874, a branch dropped from the tree witnessed by an old forester who cried: "The laird's died now!". Sure enough, Fox Maule Ramsay, the eleventh Earl of Dalhousie, was dead.

As we have read, the oak was strongly connected to the thunder gods of ancient pantheons. This linked the oak, like many other trees, to lightning and fire, in particular because it was believed that the oak was struck by lightning more than any other tree.

Indeed, Fowler's experiments in Europe, suggest that oaks are struck by lightning at a higher frequency.

In some Christian traditions, it was thought Judas hung himself from an oak and that the tree was best avoided in lightning storms.

Further lightning traditions surrounding the oak include planting oaks near a farm to attract the lightning away from thatched roofs (England and northern Europe) or placing an acorn for protection in the window (Scandinavia).

From lightning to fire, oak wood was often used for ritual fires, such as the Beltane fire, so the association is obvious.

In Germany, for example, farmers burnt oak wood for the midsummer fires on 21 June. Like the beech, the oak too was burned as the Yule log

Like many sacred trees, the oak was often used for divination. This practice was called '*dendromancy*' when seers sought the aid of a tree spirit or power.

The oak oracle was spoken by priestesses called Peleiade, or 'holy doves', who listened to the tree's rustling leaves. Their cult declined after the sacred site was plundered in 219 BC and eventually Christianised in the 4th-5th centuries.

Other oak oracles included Praeneste, which used letters cut from an oak tree to tell prophecy; the oak priestesses at Delos, who foretold the future from a gurgling spring near an oak; and the famous oracle at Delphi, where the oldest holy tree may have been the oak - later replaced by the laurel, which reflected Zeus being replaced by the laurel-god Apollo.

In Celtic traditions, acorns were eaten to gain visions of the future and the oak formed the seventh tree in the Ogham alphabet, *Duir* or 'D'.

As recently as the late 20th century, the oak, along with the ash, was used as a predictor of the weather and the harvest.

An old country charm also instructed placing two acorns in a dish of water. If the acorns floated together it predicted a love affair, but if they pushed apart it meant there would be no marriage.

In general, acorns were collected for magic charms to bring luck, health and protection.

As a magical tree, the oak was linked to the otherworld of fairies and supernatural creatures - as indeed was any plant, big or small, that was believed to have magical properties. Various charms and rituals involving the tree could be used to protect mortals from fairy enchantment.

Scottish Highlanders, for example, would draw a circle around themselves with an oak sapling to scare away fairy folk. In later Christian traditions, the oak was one of the trees used to 'beat the bounds' of the parish borders.

In fertility traditions, the oak could not only enhance people's fertility but was seen as an aphrodisiac as well. This is not surprising given that the thunder god Thor or Donar was also associated with fertility.

One oak tree in Surrey, England, called the CrouchOak, was almost killed by lovesick women peeling its bark for love potions. Railings were put around the tree to protect it.

Naturally, oak wood lent itself for use as maypoles as a symbol of fertility and love.

Oak leaves have also been connected to the Green Man of May Day, who is a pre-eminent supernatural being of Celtic traditions.

Oak Apple Day fell on May 29th at which time people wore an oak decoration in memory of King Charles II's escape.

Wedding ceremonies were often performed under 'marriage oaks'. And in the language of flowers, an oak leaf says: "Don't lose hope. Love will triumph".

Acorns too had an erotic power and classical writers claimed "the acorn was said to stimulate Venus". In art, acorns have been used to represent phallic symbols - both male and female - and to symbolise fertility.

This is illustrated in a set of German playing cards from around 1500, de Cleene and Lejeune say: "acorns were often depicted, some of which have an unmistakable connection to love (heart) and sexuality. As a matter of fact, on these old playing cards, one of the four 'suits' was the image of an acorn".

Many sacred trees have become emblems in more recent times. The oak has been a symbol of military power and royalty. The court of King Louis IX (1214-1270) of France was held in the shadow of an oak. The Parisian guardsmen also received an oak branch from Louis IX to distinguish their status; the oak emblem is still worn on the lapel of Parisian police officers today.

In England, King Charles II (1630-1685) and the battle of Worcester in 1641 features an oak 'worthy of mention'. The king hid from parliament in a hollow oak in the forest and at night he slept in a hunting lodge. When he returned to the throne, the royal oak was depicted on the coat of arms of English warships.

The 'Royal Oak' is still a popular sign found outside English pubs and shops, often with a likeness of Charles II. The oak has featured on many emblems in England, and indeed the tree itself is an unofficial emblem for the country.

For example, the English sixpenny and shilling coins were decorated on one side by a spray of oak, which was eventually replaced by the British lion.

The oak is also the national tree of England and other countries including Ireland, Albania, Finland and Germany. As a symbol of strength, it features in much heraldry.

In Germany, the oak came to symbolise peace. Oak trees have been planted in recent times in remembrance of a person who has died or as an emblem of peace after a battle.

The oak was such a powerful symbol of the old gods that Christian figures sometimes cut down these sacred trees.

Anslem (1250-1278), the bishop of Ermland, cut down a god-oak in Prussia. In Geismar, near Fritzlar in Hessen,

Germany, an oak dedicated to Thor was felled by St Boniface (674-754) in 742. Boniface built a chapel from its wood dedicated to St Peter.

In Scandinavia, oaks were 'turned' away from pagan deities, such as Thor, to Christianity by carving a cross on the trunk.

In Belarus, a wall was built around 'divine oaks' which became a shrine with a priest presiding over rituals and sacrifices. A holy oak stood in the courtyard and was only visited by the priest or by people threatened with death.

The oaks of Celtic Ireland sometimes became the sites of churches and cloisters when the country converted from paganism to Christianity. For example, County Kildare means 'the church of the oak'.

The classic 'Mary oaks' of German-speaking countries, and in France and Italy, sprung from legends that a likeness of the Virgin Mary was found on the trunk of an oak by a shepherd or other humble person. The oak then became the site of a chapel or place of pilgrimage in honour of the Mother of God.

In the Italian countryside people sometimes claimed to see imprints of the Holy Virgin on oak stumps in the 19th century, which is where the name 'Lady of the Oak' originates.

One particular miracle oak attached to the figure of Mary was at Scherpenheuvel, in the Flemish region of Belgium. The site was a place of oak-worship and pilgrimage. The tree was said to have grown into the shape of a cross, its bark could cure sickness and ward off disaster, and people hung their canes upon its branches to show that it had cured them.

The oak was Christianised by attaching a statue of the Virgin Mary to it, which in turn developed miraculous powers. The idea seemingly being that processions to visit the tree became processions to honour the statue instead.

Thus, the miracles of the oak became the miracles of Mary. The statue disappeared in 1580 - perhaps stolen by Protestants - but people still continued to visit the tree.

A chapel was eventually erected on the site and in 1603, the miracle oak was felled on the order of Bishop Miraeus of Antwerp to put a stop to the superstitions concerning the tree.

Nevertheless, the legend of the miracle oak of Scherpenheuvel survived. Pilgrims took pieces of its bark to make remedies for sickness; a piece of the 'miracle wood' was given to Archduchess Isabella (1566-1633), governess of the Netherlands; and in the church itself above the altar is a bronze image of an oak, while on the walls of a nearby well is depicted a stone image of an oak with a statue of the Virgin Mary.

These vestiges of oak-worship could not be easily erased and echoes of the tree's ancient cults were seen in Christian processions as recently as the 20th century, and perhaps still today.

A church in Tongerlo, in Antwerp, Belgium, has held several processions to carry a statue of the Virgin Mary. The tradition harks back to an oak, upon which hung a statue of Mary, which once stood at the crossroads of Tongerlo to Geel.

The oak makes several appearances in the Bible. In the Old Testament the names elah, allah, elon or allon are thought to mean a stately tree, which translators suggest meets the description of an oak, or Terebinth.

An oak is mentioned in the sanctuary of Jehovah (Joshua 24:26), but the prophets condemn oak-worship by the Israelites in Hosea 4:13, Ezekiel 6:13 and Isiah 1:29. There are many more examples of biblical oaks, such as the famous Oak of Mamre, also known as Abram's Oak in Hebron, which was believed to grow on the spot where Abraham pitched his tent.

Superstition tells us that anyone who harms the tree will lose their firstborn son. In some Christian traditions, it was said that Christ died on an oak cross, although the crucifixion wood is attributed to many other trees as well.

In places where the oak could not be Christianised, however, the faithful simply thought of other ways to turn people against pagan beliefs. Rumours were spread that oaks were evil trees inhabited by devils and other terrible supernatural creatures.

The oak's lobe-shaped leaves were supposedly the

handiwork of the devil who tore at the tree's crown with his claws.

Witches allegedly boiled oak leaves in a pan to cause storm and hail. A witch trial is recorded of a witch accused with teaching a woman how to kill a cow by breaking an oak twig and placing the pieces upon the animal. Nevertheless, the oak was also seen as a protection against sorcery - a common theme in the plant world.

Farmer's wives would put oak leaves in a milking pail when a heifer carried her first calf to prevent the milk from being stolen, likely by supernatural means.

Oak leaves had a reputation for driving away snakes and "all kinds of fantastic creatures". For a long time after the Christianisation of the oak, the superstitious made the usual charms of crosses from oak twigs and leaves or acorns were strategically placed on auspicious dates to protect against the various evils that beset mankind; such charms were not unlike those obtained from other trees and plants.

Despite the church's best efforts then, belief in the sacred oak continued until at least the 12th century and remnants of the old ways survived in some of the 'holy oaks' that still stood by the 18th-19th centuries. A holy oak in a forest near the German town of Wormeln was still the site of an annual procession in the 19th century.

Sacred trees often lend their names to places, such as eik (oak) in the place-names of Flemish boroughs and hamlets:

Jezus-Eik (Jesus-Oak), Zeveneken (Seven Oaks), and Eeklo (Oak Forest).

In Bavaria, Germany, where oak woods, Loh, once stood are place names such as Spannloh and Eberloh, or haunted places were young people are warned not to go. In England, we have Cressage in Shropshire, which was originally Cristesache, or Christ's Oak in the Domesday Book.

6

HOW TO DRY AND STORE ACORNS

Always gather your acorns green. This way the acorns are likely not to have been infested by larvae, beetles and rodents.

Take the acorn out of the cup and lay flat in single layers on a drying sheet, tabletop and allow to dry. They are ready when they sound like they have a bean inside them.

Store the dried acorns in their shell in large buckets with an airtight lid.

The secret is to get them very dry and store them in their shells because the tannin is a natural preservative.

7

HOW TO PROCESS ACORNS

METHOD 1

You can either process acorns fresh (green shell) or dried (brown shell).

First, you need to remove the nut from the shell. The easiest way is to split them in half using a knife. Then pop the nut out.

Discard any damaged nuts.

Put the nuts into a food processor with enough cold water to cover. Never use hot water at any stage when processing acorns. Then pulse until you get a mash, next pour the mixture into a large jar or bucket.

Place the jar under a tap (or use a hose) and allow the water to circulate and gently overspill for between 1-2- minutes.

Slowly stir the mixture. While doing this make sure the mash doesn't come out.

Pour off the water and refill one last time. Then cover the jar to prevent dust and insects entering.

Each day, pour off the dark tannin water and refill. Make sure you don't pour away the fine starch in the bottom of the jar or bucket. Refill with cold water.

Stir twice a day throughout the leaching process.

Acorns can take anything from 2 to 10 days to remove the tannin depending on what species of oak used.

Once the leaching is complete. Spread the mash in layers no thicker than 1 cm on a baking tray. Then place in an oven at the lowest setting leaving the door slightly ajar.

Turn the mash every hour breaking up any clumps that have formed. Once dry (takes around 12 hours) cool before storing

in sealed jars.

Blend the mash until it becomes flour. The flour will store in sealed bags in the freezer for up to 2 years.

METHOD 2

Slice each acorn in half, and pop the nut out into a bucket.

Fill with cold water and cover to keep dust and insects out. Stir twice a day.

Each day pour off the water and replace with fresh cold water. Repeat until the nuts taste sweet and you feel most of the tannin has been removed.

Acorns leached this way can take anything from 2 to 14 days to remove the tannin depending on what species of oak used. Let your tastebuds tell you when they are done.

Once leached spread out the halved acorn nuts in single layers on sheets and dry in a low-temperature oven leaving the oven door slightly ajar. Takes around 12 hours, maybe longer. Or dry in a dehydrator.

When completely dry, place in halved acorns in an airtight sealed container and freeze for later use.

SPICED PICKLED ACORNS

- 550g whole/halved acorns
- 6tsp sea salt
- 500ml malt vinegar
- 150g sugar
- ½tsp ground black pepper
- ½tsp ground allspice
- ½tsp ground cloves
- ½tsp ground cinnamon
- 1tbsp freshly grated ginger

Cover acorns in salted water for 24 hours. Strain and allow to air dry for a few hours. In a pan add the black pepper, allspice, cloves, cinnamon, grated ginger and malt vinegar. Bring to boil then simmer for 10 minutes. Spoon acorns into jars, then cover with the spiced vinegar and seal.

If you get twitchy you can eat them after 14 days, but they are best if allowed to mature for between 3-6 months.

GATHER CLUB BONUS GIFTS

Join my Gather Club and receive a photo identification guide which includes 18 full colour photos.

You'll also receive a free copy of my Stinging Nettle Notebook.

All bonus gifts are delivered to your inbox as PDF files. You can access the material on a mobile, tablet or computer - even without internet access.

It's completely free to sign up and you will never be spammed by me. You can easily opt out any time.

To join the Gather Club, visit

eatweeds.co.uk/oak-notebook

PLEASE LEAVE A REVIEW!

If you have enjoyed this book, it would be tremendous if you could leave a review.

Reviews help me gain visibility and they can bring my books to the attention of other readers who may enjoy them.

To leave a review please visit Amazon.

Thank you!

MORE BOOKS FROM ROBIN HARFORD

Robin Harford is a plant-based forager, ethnobotanical researcher and wild food educator.

He has published over 40 foraging guide books, visit -

eatweeds.co.uk/foraging-guide-books

ABOUT THE AUTHOR

Robin Harford is a professional forager, ethnobotanical researcher, wild food educator and sensory botanist.

He gathers wild edible plants on a daily basis, and is the creator of the UK's leading wild food site eatweeds.co.uk, which is listed in The Times Top 50 websites for food and drink.

Robin has been writing, filming, publishing and teaching people about their local edible landscape since 2008. Recently his foraging courses where voted #1 in the country by BBC Countryfile.

He is also a co-director of Plants & Healers International, a non-profit that connects people, plants and healers around the world.

He travels extensively documenting and recording the traditional and local uses of wild food plants in indigenous cultures, and his work has taken him to Africa, India, SE Asia, Europe and the USA.

Robin has taught foraging at Eden Project, appeared on BBC2's Edwardian Farm, Soul Seekers TV series, appeared on national and local BBC radio and been recommended in BBC Good Food magazine, Sainsbury's magazine as well as in The Guardian, The Times, The Independent, The Daily Telegraph, GQ, The Ecologist and Green Parent, to name a few.

Follow him on social media -

facebook.com/foragingcourses

instagram.com/robinjharford

Eatweeds
47 Old Abbey Court
Salmon Pool Lane,
Exeter, EX1 2DS
United Kingdom

www.eatweeds.co.uk

BIBLIOGRAPHY

Allen, D. E. & Hatfield, G. (2004) *Medicinal Plants in Folk Tradition: An Ethnobotany of Britain & Ireland.* Portland, OR: Timber Press.

Baker, M. L. (2008) *Discovering the Folklore of Plants.* Oxford: Shire.

Bartram, T. (1998) *Bartram's Encyclopedia of Herbal Medicine.* New York: Marlowe.

Cleene, M. de & Lejeune, M. C. (2002) *Compendium of Symbolic and Ritual Plants in Europe.* Ghent: Man & Culture.

Conway, P. (2002) *Tree Medicine: A Comprehensive Guide to the Healing Power of Over 170 Trees.* London: Piatkus.

Couplan, F. (1998) *The Encyclopedia of Edible Plants of North America.* New Canaan, Conn: Keats Pub.

Culpeper, N. (1995) *Culpeper's Complete Herbal: A Book of Natural Remedies for Ancient Ills*. Wordsworth reference. Ware: Wordsworth Editions.

Duke, J. A. & Duke, J. A. (2002) *Handbook of Medicinal Herbs*. 2nd ed. Boca Raton, FL: CRC Press.

Elias, T. S. & Dykeman, P. A. (2009) *Edible Wild Plants: A North American Field Guide to Over 200 Natural Foods*. New York: Sterling.

Facciola, S. (1998) *Cornucopia II: A Source Book of Edible Plants*. Vista, CA: Kampong Publications.

Fernald, M. L. et al. (1996) *Edible Wild Plants of Eastern North America*. New York: Dover Publications.

Folkard, R. F. (2017) *Plant lore, Legends, and Lyrics.: Embracing the Myths, Traditions, superstitions, and folk-lore of the plant Kingdom*. hansebooks.

Gardner, Z. E. et al. (eds.) (2013) *American Herbal Products Association's Botanical Safety Handbook*. 2nd ed. Boca Raton: American Herbal Products Association, CRC Press.

Gibbons, E. (1987) *Stalking the Wild Asparagus*. 25th anniversary ed. Putney, Vt.: Woodstock, Vt: A.C. Hood; Distributed by the Countryman Press.

Grieve, M. & Leyel, C. F. (1998) *A Modern Herbal: The Medical, Culinary, Cosmetic and Economic Properties, Cultivation and Folklore of Herbs, Grasses, Fungi, Shrubs and Trees and All Their Modern Scientific Uses*. London: Tiger Books International.

Grigson, G. (1996) *The Englishman's Flora*. Oxford: Helicon.

Haines, A. (n.d.) *Ancestral Plants: A Primitive Skills Guide to Important Edible, Medicinal, and Useful Plants of the Northwest, Volume 2*. Korea: Anaskimin.

Hatfield, G. (2008) *Hatfield's Herbal: The Secret History of British Plants*. London: Penguin.

Hu, S. (2005) *Food Plants of China*. Hong Kong: Chinese University Press.

Karalliedde, L. et al. (2008) *Traditional Herbal Medicines: A Guide to Their Safer Use*. London: Hammersmith.

Kuhnlein, H. V. & Turner, N. J. (1991) *Traditional Plant Foods of Canadian Indigenous Peoples: Nutrition, Botany, and Use*. Food and nutrition in history and anthropology v. 8. Philadelphia: Gordon and Breach.

Kunkel, G. (1984) *Plants for Human Consumption: An Annotated Checklist of the Edible Phanerogams and Ferns*. Koenigstein: Koeltz Scientific Books.

Łuczaj, Ł. & Szymański, W. M. (2007) Wild Vascular Plants Gathered for Consumption in the Polish Countryside: A Review. *Journal of Ethnobiology and Ethnomedicine*. [Online] 3 (1), 17.

Mabey, R. & Blamey, M. (1974) *Food for Free*. London: Collins.

Mac Coitir, N. & Langrishe, G. (2015) *Ireland's Wild Plants: Myths, Legends and Folklore.*

Manandhar, N. P. & Manandhar, S. (2002) *Plants and People of Nepal.* Portland, OR: Timber Press.

Menendez-Baceta, G. et al. (2012) Wild Edible Plants Traditionally Gathered in Gorbeialdea (biscay, Basque Country). *Genetic Resources and Crop Evolution.* [Online] 59 (7), 1329–1347.

Pennacchio, M. et al. (2010) *Uses and Abuses of Plant-Derived Smoke: It's Ethnobotany as Hallucinogen, Perfume, Incense, and Medicine.* New York, N.Y: Oxford University Press.

Pulsipher, L. M. & Kermath, B. (n.d.) *Food Plants in the Americas: A Survey of the Domesticated, Cultivated, and Wild Plants Used for Human Food in North, Central and South America and the Caribbean.*

Quattrocchi, U. (2012) CRC World Dictionary of Medicinal and Poisonous Plants: Common Names, Scientific Names, Eponyms, Synonyms, and Etymology. Boca Raton, Fla: CRC.

Simkova, K. & Polesny, Z. (2015) Ethnobotanical review of wild edible plants used in the Czech Republic. *Journal of Applied Botany and Food Quality.* 88.

Smith, J. R. (2016) *Tree Crops: A Permanent Agriculture.*

Sõukand, R. & Kalle, R. (2016) *Changes in the Use of Wild Food Plants in Estonia 18th - 21st Century.* Cham: Springer International Publishing.

Sturtevant, E. L. (1972) Sturtevant's Edible Plants of the World. New York: Dover Publications.

Thayer, S. (2010) *Nature's Garden: A Guide to Identifying, Harvesting, and Preparing Edible Wild Plants*. Birchwood, WI: Forager's Harvest.

Uphof, J. C. T. (1959) *Dictionary of Economic Plants*. New York: H R Engelmann.

Usher, G. (1974) *A Dictionary of Plants Used by Man*. London: Constable.

Vickery, R. (1995) *A Dictionary of Plant-Lore*. Oxford: Oxford University Press.

Warren, P. (2006) *British Native Trees: Their Past and Present Uses: Including a Guide to Burning Wood in the Home*. Dereham: Wildeye.

Watts, D. (2007) *Dictionary of Plant Lore*. Amsterdam; Boston: Elsevier/AP.

Wiersema, J. H. & León, B. (2013) *World Economic Plants: A Standard Reference*. 2nd ed. Boca Raton, Fla.: CRC Press.

Wyse Jackson, P. (2013) *Ireland's Generous Nature: The Past and Present Uses of Wild Plants in Ireland*. St. Louis, MO: Missouri Botanical Garden Press.

Printed in Poland
by Amazon Fulfillment
Poland Sp. z o.o., Wrocław

50160063R00042